OVERCOMING ADVERSITY:
SHARING THE AMERICAN DREAM

# ROSA PARKS

**MASON CREST PUBLISHERS**
**PHILADELPHIA**

OVERCOMING ADVERSITY:
SHARING THE AMERICAN DREAM

Charles Barkley

Halle Berry

Cesar Chavez

Kenny Chesney

George Clooney

Johnny Depp

Tony Dungy

Jermaine Dupri

Jennifer Garner

Kevin Garnett

John B. Herrington

Salma Hayek

Vanessa Hudgens

Samuel L. Jackson

Norah Jones

Martin Lawrence

Bruce Lee

Eva Longoria

Malcolm X

Carlos Mencia

Chuck Norris

Barack Obama

Rosa Parks

Bill Richardson

Russell Simmons

Carrie Underwood

Modern American
  Indian Leaders

OVERCOMING ADVERSITY:
SHARING THE AMERICAN DREAM

# ROSA PARKS

**SUSAN HOE**

**MASON CREST PUBLISHERS**
**PHILADELPHIA**

# ABOUT CROSS-CURRENTS

When you see this logo, turn to the Cross-Currents section at the back of the book. The Cross-Currents features explore connections between people, places, events, and ideas.

Produced by OTTN Publishing, Stockton, New Jersey

**Mason Crest Publishers**
370 Reed Road
Broomall, PA 19008
www.masoncrest.com

First printing

1  3  5  7  9  8  6  4  2


Library of Congress Cataloging-in-Publication Data

Hoe, Susan.
  Rosa Parks / Susan Hoe.
      p. cm. — (Sharing the American dream : overcoming adversity)
   ISBN 978-1-4222-0597-6 (hardcover) — ISBN 978-1-4222-0760-4 (pbk.)
 1.  Parks, Rosa, 1913-2005--Juvenile literature. 2.  African American
women—Alabama—Montgomery—Biography—Juvenile literature. 3.  African
Americans—Alabama—Montgomery—Biography—Juvenile literature. 4.  Civil rights
workers—Alabama—Montgomery—Biography—Juvenile literature. 5.  African
Americans—Civil rights—Alabama—Montgomery—History—20th century—Juvenile literature. 6.  Segregation in transportation—Alabama—Montgomery—History—20th
century—Juvenile literature. 7.  Montgomery (Ala.)—Race relations—Juvenile literature. 8.
Montgomery (Ala.)—Biography—Juvenile literature. I. Title.
  F334.M753P3844 2008
  323.092--dc22
  [B]
                                                2008028906

OVERCOMING ADVERSITY:
SHARING THE AMERICAN DREAM

# TABLE OF CONTENTS

Chapter One: Ending Bus Segregation
   in Montgomery      **6**

Chapter Two: A Child of the South    **13**

Chapter Three: Sitting Down for
   Her Rights     **20**

Chapter Four: The Montgomery Bus
   Boycott     **28**

Chapter Five: Working for Civil Rights   **36**

Cross-Currents    **46**

Chronology    **54**

Accomplishments/Awards    **56**

Further Reading    **57**

Internet Resources    **57**

Glossary    **58**

Chapter Notes    **59**

Index    **61**

# CHAPTER ONE

# ENDING BUS SEGREGATION IN MONTGOMERY

Empty yellow buses rumbled through the streets of Montgomery, Alabama, on a dreary December morning in 1956. For more than a year, buses that should have been crowded with people going to and from work had traveled their routes with just a few passengers.

On December 1, 1955, a middle-aged African American woman named Rosa Parks had stepped onto the Cleveland Avenue bus on her way home from work. In Montgomery, segregation on buses was the law. This meant that black people had to sit in the back or give up their seats to whites. But Rosa had refused to give up her seat to a white passenger, and she'd been arrested. In protest, the African American community had banded together and organized a boycott of the bus company. Black people refused to ride Montgomery's buses.

In mid-November 1956, the U.S. Supreme Court ruled that the separation of blacks and whites in public places, such as buses, was unconstitutional and illegal. Blacks had the right to ride Montgomery buses as equals. There could no longer be a section for blacks and a section for whites, and people of all races were entitled to keep the seat they occupied. But the city didn't immediately move to end segregation on buses, so the federal

Rosa Parks, circa December 1955. In the background is Martin Luther King Jr., leader of the Montgomery bus boycott.

government issued an order on December 20 that forced Montgomery to follow the Supreme Court decision. The following day, leaders of the bus boycott were scheduled to ride Montgomery buses to mark the victory.

## Riding the Bus Again

Rosa Parks, the person who had started it all, didn't plan to join the leaders of the boycott in their celebratory gesture. However, reporters who were covering this watershed event urged her to ride with them, and Rosa consented. She slowly stepped onto one of the buses and took a seat in the front. As she sat there staring out the window, the events of the past year played through her mind like a movie.

The year of the boycott had been a difficult one, not only for Rosa Parks and her family but also for the entire African American community in Montgomery. Nevertheless, the first step had been taken to end segregation. Yet Rosa knew as well as anyone that the struggle for equality had just begun. While the law was now on the side of African Americans on the issue of bus segregation, there would be other laws to change and other issues to address. And the African American community was opposed by people with hard hearts and closed minds. "I suspect that he never did change his attitude about African Americans and how we should be treated," Rosa would write of the bus driver who had forced her arrest a year earlier. "Many people do not want to change, which is why it was so important for us to at least get the laws changed so we would have some protection."

It would take years before full civil rights were guaranteed to African Americans under the law—and longer still for prejudices to slowly begin disappearing. Negative attitudes toward blacks were deeply entrenched in American society, with roots going back to the practice of slavery.

## Coming from Slavery

Slavery existed throughout Britain's North American colonies before the American Revolution. The first colony to legalize slavery was Massachusetts, in 1641. Slaves were captured in Africa, transported across the Atlantic Ocean in chains, and then sold in the colonies.

Through the Revolutionary War, the American colonies secured their independence from Great Britain and became the United States. But while the Declaration of Independence had stated the "self-evident" truths "that all Men are created equal, that they are endowed by their Creator with certain Unalienable Rights" such as "Life, Liberty, and the Pursuit of Happiness," America's Founding Fathers didn't end slavery. The U.S. Constitution, which was drafted in 1787, merely gave Congress the authority to stop the importation of slaves into

The human cargo of a slave ship. Scholars estimate that disease and malnutrition claimed the lives of 10 to 20 percent of captive Africans during a typical voyage across the Atlantic Ocean. Those who survived were sold into slavery once they reached the Western Hemisphere.

the country after 1807. The slave trade was, in fact, outlawed as of January 1, 1808.

By then all the Northern states had passed laws to end slavery, although it would be some time before all the individuals already enslaved were freed. In the South, meanwhile, slavery became more and more important. The economies of the Southern states depended on agriculture. The most important crops, such as cotton, tobacco, and rice, were grown on large plantations. Slaves provided the labor.

Slaves had no rights, and most were not allowed to learn how to read. They were considered the property of the plantation owners, like a chair or a horse. Even so, black slaves formed a community of their own. They married and had families. But to slave owners, these people were possessions. Slave families were often ripped apart when a father, mother, sister, or brother was sold to another owner who lived many miles away.

Slaves living on a plantation in South Carolina, circa 1862.

The Civil War (1861–1865) was fought, in part, over the issue of slavery. The Southern plantation owners wanted to keep their slaves, whom they needed to work their large fields. Most Northerners looked upon slavery as an evil and wanted the government to pass laws forbidding slavery altogether.

At the height of the Civil War, on January 1, 1863, President Abraham Lincoln issued the Emancipation Proclamation, which declared slaves within the rebel Confederate states free. Following the end of the Civil War and the death of President Lincoln, Congress passed and the states ratified the Thirteenth Amendment to the U.S. Constitution, which outlawed slavery throughout the United States. All freed slaves were now able to move about wherever they chose.

**READ MORE**

The Emancipation Proclamation of 1863 declared that all slaves within the rebellious Confederate states were free. But it didn't immediately free those slaves. Turn to page 46 for details.

## The Black Codes and Jim Crow

To limit the activities and movement of freed slaves—now called freedmen—Southern states passed the Black Codes. Under these state laws, the freed slaves were treated as an inferior group. They were no longer slaves, but they did not have the same rights as whites. Freedmen were subject to unfair laws that said if they didn't have a job or a place to live, they could be arrested and fined—or worse yet, sent to work in plantation fields. There were limits to the type of property and businesses that freedmen could own. They were not allowed to carry guns, and marriage with a non-black was illegal.

To counter the Black Code laws, Congress passed the Civil Rights Act of 1866, which tried to establish and safeguard the rights of freed slaves. However, it was uncertain whether this act

In the years after the Civil War, violence against former slaves was common in the South. This woodcut depicts an incident that occurred in New Orleans in July 1866. A white mob attacked a group of freedmen going to a political convention, killing 40.

could be enforced, so Congress passed the Fourteenth Amendment to the U.S. Constitution. It granted citizenship to all people born or naturalized in the United States. This included all freed slaves. The amendment forbade any state to "deprive any person of life, liberty, or property, without due process of law; nor deny to any person . . . equal protection of the laws."

Congress also established the Freedmen's Bureau. This organization was supposed to help former slaves make the transition into their new free life. The bureau provided food and medical help to the 4 million freed slaves. One of the most important goals of the bureau was to set up schools to educate the African Americans, who were mostly unable to read.

Despite the federal government's measures to counter the Black Codes, Southern states found ways to keep blacks from enjoying equality with whites. By the late 1870s, the Southern states had once again devised local laws that would keep African Americans segregated from whites in public places and in schools. These laws were called Jim Crow laws.

When Rosa Parks was born, the Jim Crow laws were still in effect. They not only separated African Americans physically from the white community, but also kept blacks from moving up in life.

READ MORE

Turn to page 47 for additional information about the Jim Crow laws.

# CHAPTER TWO

# A CHILD OF THE SOUTH

When Rosa Louise McCauley was born on February 4, 1913, in Tuskegee, Alabama, she lived in a part of the South where Jim Crow laws were strictly enforced. Even though Tuskegee was home to the Tuskegee Institute, a well-known industrial college for African Americans, the town was still highly segregated. Black citizens had their own schools, churches, and restaurants.

Rosa's father, James McCauley, was a carpenter. Her mother, Leona Edwards McCauley, was a teacher. Rosa's younger brother, Sylvester, was born in 1915. When her husband left the family to find work elsewhere, Leona McCauley moved with her children to Pine Level, Alabama, to live with her parents.

Leona found a teaching job in Spring Hill, a small town about eight miles away. During the week Leona remained in Spring Hill, while Rosa and her brother stayed with their grandparents. Money was scarce. The little amount that Leona brought home was used for clothing and other essentials. Fortunately, because the family lived on a farm, there was plenty of food to eat.

To help support the family, Rosa and her brother went to work on a nearby cotton plantation when they were still very young. During harvest season, Rosa and Sylvester worked among the rows of cotton, picking the fluffy little balls from the prickly plants. It was extremely hot working under the searing sun. Rosa remembered how they were sometimes beaten when they pricked their little fingers and accidentally smeared some blood on the pure white cotton.

## Going to School

When the harvest season was over, Rosa and Sylvester attended school. It was a small one-room schoolhouse that sat on the grounds of the African Methodist Episcopal church. There was only one teacher for about 50 students, all of whom were black. The students learned the basics of reading, writing, and arithmetic.

Although the African American students had a school of their own, it was very primitive in comparison to the schools that the

Students in a one-room, all-black schoolhouse, Muskogee, Oklahoma, circa 1917. During the Jim Crow era, the schools that black children attended were often run-down and overcrowded.

white students in the nearby community attended. Rosa's school was made of wood and only had shutters over the windows. The town provided no heat in the winter. There was a wood stove in the classroom, but the students had to bring their own wood to burn in order to have heat.

The school that the white students attended was made of bricks and had glass windows. It was well heated in the winter. Also, these students were transported to school on buses, while Rosa and the other black students had to walk to school. Sometimes white students riding past in the bus threw their garbage at the black kids who were walking to school.

## Night Terrors

By the time Rosa was six years old, many African American soldiers were returning from Europe after fighting in World War I. They came home with a renewed sense of hope. After serving their country, they expected their rights as citizens to be recognized and improved. But that did not happen. Instead, they were met with more violence—from the Ku Klux Klan, a group of white citizens who hated blacks and did not intend to allow them to improve their lot in life. The Klan rampaged through black

**READ MORE**

For a brief history of the notorious Ku Klux Klan, turn to page 48.

neighborhoods, burning homes, churches, and businesses. They terrorized the people, including young Rosa. Sometimes, Klan members grabbed innocent black men and murdered them, leaving their bodies hanging from trees. Rosa remembered many nights when her grandfather sat in the darkened living room holding a rifle, just in case the Klan came to their home to cause trouble.

Hooded members of the Ku Klux Klan burst into the home of a black family. The Klan often attacked its victims at night.

During their childhood, Rosa and her brother had several unpleasant encounters with white children and adults. Not understanding the possible consequences, Rosa sometimes talked back to whites who harassed them. Rosa's grandmother warned her against this. She told Rosa never to retaliate if a white person did something to her. Although Rosa listened to her grandmother's words, the feisty young girl felt that "I was very much in my rights to try to defend myself if I could."

## Moving to Montgomery

When Rosa was about 11, the little schoolhouse she attended closed. There were no other schools in the area for African American children. Leona decided to send Rosa and Sylvester to Montgomery, Alabama, to live with relatives and go to school there. It was a big change for the girl from tiny Pine Level. Montgomery was a large, bustling city with a community of educated, middle-class African Americans, including doctors, lawyers, professors, and successful businessmen.

But even in a city with a black professional class, Rosa quickly became aware of the not-so-invisible lines that were drawn between blacks and whites. Something as small as a public water fountain was governed by the Jim Crow laws—with fountains marked for "coloreds" and fountains marked for "whites." Seeing the signs for the first time, Rosa wondered if the water came in different colors.

## Going to School in Montgomery

In Montgomery, Rosa enrolled in the Montgomery Industrial School, also known as Miss White's School for Girls after its cofounder and principal, Miss Alice L. White. While all of the school's students were black, Miss White and all of the other teachers were white women from the North. Associating with African Americans meant that Miss White and the other teachers were excluded from the white community in Montgomery. In business for just a few years before Rosa started, Miss White's School had already been set afire at least two times.

Leona initially paid for Rosa's tuition, but as times got even harder, Rosa was given a scholarship. In payment, she did minor cleaning jobs at the school such as emptying trash cans and sweeping the floor.

While at Miss White's, Rosa took classes in English, science, geography, and math, as well as "domestic science"—a course for young girls. In domestic science, the girls learned how to cook, sew, and care for the sick. This last class was very important to the

A water fountain for blacks in Halifax, North Carolina, circa 1938. Jim Crow laws kept blacks separate from whites in all spheres of public life.

community because African Americans were not allowed in hospitals. They had to be cared for at home by women who had some knowledge of medical care. Rosa also became quite a good seamstress, a talent she would call upon in later years. But even more important than practical matters, Miss White's School reinforced in Rosa a lesson her mother and grandparents had tried to instill in her as a child. It taught her, Rosa would later write, "that I was a person with dignity and self-respect, and I should not set my sights lower than anybody else just because I was black. We were taught to be ambitious and to believe that we could do what we wanted in life."

After Miss White's School closed, Rosa attended another all-black school, Booker T. Washington Junior High. When she was ready for high school, there were no public high schools for blacks, so she went to the Alabama State Teachers' College for Negroes. When she was about to enter the 11th grade in 1929, Rosa's grandmother became ill and Rosa dropped out of school and returned to Pine Level to care for her.

Soon after Rosa's grandmother died, her mother also became ill, and Rosa went to work to earn some money for the family. She didn't finish high school then, but returned five years later.

## Marriage and Dangerous Times

In 1931, Rosa was introduced to Raymond Parks, a barber. Confident and intelligent, Parks impressed Rosa, who would call him a "person who inspired me, because he believed in freedom and equality himself." He was also, Rosa said, the first activist she had ever met. Parks was a member of the NAACP, the National Association for the Advancement of Colored People.

In 1932, Rosa and Raymond Parks were married at her mother's home in Pine Level. She then decided she wanted to go back to school to get her high school diploma, which she did in 1934.

Around this time, Raymond Parks was working to help raise money for the legal defense of nine African Americans known as the Scottsboro Boys. In 1931, the nine teens had been accused of raping two white women on a train. Although there was little evidence to support the accusations, all-white juries in Scottsboro, Alabama, convicted the black youths after hasty trials. Eight of the nine defendants were sentenced to death; jurors couldn't decide whether the youngest should be executed or sentenced to life imprisonment.

Raymond Parks stepped forward in support of the Scottsboro Boys' legal appeals. It was dangerous work. Angry whites threatened to beat Parks up or even kill him for his activities. But Parks believed in what he was doing and showed a lot of courage.

To plan their strategies, people working on the case met at different homes each night. One evening, when it was Raymond Parks's turn to host the meeting, Rosa was frightened to see pistols and rifles piled on one of her tables in the living room. Although the firearms were only for protection, Rosa was terrified by the possibility of violence. She left the living room and went to the back porch, where she sat in silence for the rest of the evening. Not much had changed since the time her grandfather sat with his rifle in fear of a raid from the Ku Klux Klan.

Although she felt helpless and scared, Rosa was inspired

**READ MORE**

The case of the Scottsboro Boys was a shameful chapter in the long history of bias against blacks accused of crimes. Turn to page 49 to learn more about the case.

by her husband and the other activists who were willing to risk their lives for other African Americans. Rosa would soon take the first step to become a civil rights activist herself.

# CHAPTER THREE

# SITTING DOWN FOR HER RIGHTS

In 1941, Rosa Parks was working as a secretary at the Maxwell Field Army Air Force base in Montgomery, Alabama. Although U.S. military units were still segregated, President Franklin D. Roosevelt had desegregated the country's military bases. This meant that black and white employees used the same public facilities. They dined in the same cafeteria, used the same restrooms, and sat next to each other on the base trolley (bus).

For Rosa, mingling with white people was a new experience. Sometimes when she rode on the base trolley, she chatted with a white woman who lived on the base. But once outside the base, it was Jim Crow as usual. Getting on the same city bus, the white woman took her seat among the first 10 rows designated for whites, while Rosa walked to the back of the bus.

## A Volunteer for the NAACP

Living a segregated life, but experiencing what it would be like in an integrated world, Rosa decided to join the NAACP. Hopefully, she thought, she could help her fellow African Americans. In 1943, Rosa attended the annual meeting of the NAACP's Montgomery chapter. At that meeting members were electing their new officers. To Rosa's dismay, she was the only female there and was chosen as the secretary—a position that was considered a woman's job. She was too timid to decline and started taking meeting notes that very night.

Rosa worked for the NAACP for the next 12 years as a volunteer with E. D. Nixon, the chapter's president. She performed office duties, writing letters, handling membership dues, answering the phone, informing members of any upcoming events, and submitting notices to the press. It was a lot of work, but Rosa felt that she was helping the civil rights cause in her own way.

The NAACP, the oldest civil rights organization in the United States, was founded in 1909.

One of Rosa's jobs as Nixon's assistant was to document the details of incidents in Alabama involving racial discrimination or racial violence against African Americans. There were hundreds of these cases reported, but often the blacks involved became too frightened to tell their stories in detail. They feared there would be some sort of revenge set upon them by the white offenders.

As an adviser to the NAACP Youth Council, Rosa Parks organized students to take action in order to secure their education. She encouraged them to use public libraries that were supposedly for whites only.

## Standing in the Back

One of the most degrading segregation laws in Montgomery affected the public buses. Some bus drivers would force black passengers—who had just paid to get on the bus—to get off the bus and reenter from the back where blacks were allowed to sit. Mean-spirited drivers sometimes drove away before the passenger could board through the back door.

In 1943, Rosa encountered a bus driver who demanded that she board from the back door. Since the back of the bus was already filled and people were standing in the stairwell of the back door, Rosa ignored the driver and walked to the back from inside the bus. Angered by her defiance, the driver grabbed her by her coat sleeve and pulled her to the front, where Rosa sat down to pick up the purse she had dropped. Rosa thought the angry driver was about to hit her when he shouted, "Get off my bus." Defiant as ever, she said back to him, "You better not hit me." And with that she left the bus. Rosa was frustrated and angry that her fellow blacks hadn't understood what she was doing. She had heard some of them say, "How come she don't go around and get in the back? She ought to go around the back and get in."

The incident left Rosa shaken. From that time on, she always checked who the driver was before boarding the bus. She didn't want to run into the driver who had angrily confronted her.

## Registering to Vote

Although they had the right to vote in elections, many African Americans in the South couldn't exercise that right because they weren't registered. The registration process was purposefully designed to be inconvenient and difficult for blacks, to keep as many as possible from being able to vote. For example, the window of time to register was often very small—perhaps only two hours during a time of day when most African Americans were at work. In addition, black people trying to register were required to take a literacy test to prove they could read and were asked questions about the U.S. Constitution.

(White voters typically didn't have to take the test.) To prevent a black person from voting, the registration board could simply say that the person hadn't passed the test.

In 1940, Rosa had wanted to vote for President Franklin D. Roosevelt, but she had never registered to vote. She especially admired First Lady Eleanor Roosevelt. In 1939, Mrs. Roosevelt had supported the opera singer Marian Anderson, who was denied the opportunity to perform at the Daughters of the American Revolution's Constitution Hall because she was black. Several years had passed since then, and Rosa decided it was time to get registered.

She took the literacy test and felt confident she had passed, but was told she hadn't. A second attempt yielded the same result. In 1945, after taking the test for a third time, Rosa was informed that she had passed. She was 32 years old. That meant she had to pay a poll tax of $16.50—$1.50 for each of the 11 years past her 21st birthday. Although $16.50 may not sound like much today, at the time it was a significant sum, especially for a person who didn't earn much money. Like the literacy test, the poll tax was designed to minimize the number of African American voters. Rosa paid the money, however, and she voted for the first time in the 1946 Alabama governor's race. Through the Montgomery Voters League, Rosa urged

Singer Marian Anderson (right) poses for a photo with First Lady Eleanor Roosevelt after being presented with the NAACP's Spingarn Medal, 1939.

other African Americans to exercise their right to vote, and she taught them how to prepare for the voter registration process. But the high cost and the unfair tests discouraged many.

## The Highlander School

In 1954, Rosa Parks met Virginia Durr, a white woman who—along with her attorney husband Clifford Durr—often helped African Americans with legal issues. The Durrs were opponents of segregation, and they worked and socialized with black people.

That same year, the U.S. Supreme Court handed down a historic legal decision in the case called *Brown v. Board of Education*. The decision made it illegal for public school systems to maintain separate schools for whites and blacks. How segregated schools, especially in the South, would respond to the decision and start to integrate remained uncertain, however.

READ MORE

Page 50 provides details about the landmark 1954 Supreme Court decision in *Brown v. Board of Education*.

Around the time of the *Brown v. Board* decision, Virginia Durr invited Rosa Parks to a 10-day conference on civil rights that was to be held in July 1955 at the Highlander Folk School in Monteagle, Tennessee. The goal of the workshops was to develop leadership in African American groups. The school's founder, Myles Horton, believed that blacks could not passively wait and hope for the government to improve their lives. They had to take responsibility for ending segregation. "Black people," Horton said, "are going to have to force the white people to respect them. . . . The burden and the responsibility is on the whites, but the burden of change is on the blacks."

The conference at Highlander changed Rosa Parks. She came away with a heightened sense of purpose for herself and for the black community.

## A Courageous Act on the Bus

Rosa's determination to make a difference was renewed by a shocking incident that took place in Mississippi in August of 1955. Emmett Till, a 14-year-old black teen visiting from Chicago, was taken from his uncle's home, beaten, and shot to death by two white men, who dumped his body in the Tallahatchie River. Earlier, Till had whistled at the wife of one of the men. In September 1955, the men were tried in Sumner, Mississippi. The outcome was never in doubt. "Your ancestors will turn over in their grave," a defense attorney told the 12 white men on the jury, "and I'm sure every last Anglo-Saxon one of you has the courage to free these men." The jury spent just an hour in deliberations—reportedly amid laughter and refreshments—before returning a verdict of not guilty. Later, the defendants would tell a reporter for *Look* magazine how they had killed Emmett Till.

The Till tragedy—as well as other cases of violence against African Americans which Rosa Parks heard about while working for the NAACP—brought the lessons of the Highlander conference into clear focus. Rosa wouldn't wait for the government to help the African American community. When the chance came to stand up for herself and for the cause of civil rights, she was ready.

Rosa was working as a seamstress at a local department store, the Montgomery Fair. It was Thursday, December 1, 1955,

**READ MORE**

The NAACP has been working to ensure equality and eliminate discrimination in the United States for a century. To learn more about this organization, see page 51.

and she was returning home from work. She stepped onto the Cleveland Avenue bus and paid her fare. Only then did she realize that the driver was the same man who had thrown her off the bus 12 years earlier. Although there were a number of black passengers standing in the back, Rosa walked to the middle of the bus and took a seat in the first row of the black section.

At the next stop, several white riders boarded the bus and filled the remaining reserved seats. One white man was still standing. The bus driver turned toward Rosa and the other three blacks who were sitting in her row and demanded that they get up and move. The other three obeyed, but Rosa refused to rise and slid down to the window seat. When the driver asked her if she was going to move, Rosa told him she was not.

He threatened to have her arrested. She replied, "You may do that." Many people think that Rosa Parks refused to move because she was physically tired. She denied that this was the case. "I [had] made up my mind," Rosa recalled, "that I would not give in any longer to legally imposed racial segregation." At that moment she had made a conscious decision to remain and to accept whatever consequences came—which could have meant being roughed up, beaten, and arrested.

## Taken to Jail

Rosa Parks was in fact arrested. Two policemen arrived on the scene and took her away in a squad car. At Montgomery's City Hall, she was fingerprinted, photographed for mug shots, and taken to a jail cell. Rosa asked if she could use the telephone and called home. She told her mother she was in jail and asked that her husband come to get her out.

It didn't take long for Rosa's friends to learn of her arrest. By the time Raymond Parks arrived at City Hall, E. D. Nixon and Virginia and Clifford Durr had already bailed Rosa out. Later that

This police mug shot was taken in February 1956, after Rosa Parks and others were arrested for participating in the Montgomery bus boycott.

day, Nixon asked Rosa if she would be the plaintiff in a test case against the city of Montgomery. The NAACP was looking for the right person to file a suit against the city over the issue of bus segregation, and Rosa Parks met all the requirements: she was a woman with a good reputation and without a prior police record.

Rosa agreed to take on the city of Montgomery. In making that decision, she stepped out of her anonymous life and into the history books. Her actions on that Cleveland Avenue bus would mark the start of the modern-day civil rights movement.

# CHAPTER FOUR

---

# THE MONTGOMERY BUS BOYCOTT

---

Within hours of Rosa Parks's release from jail on December 1, the Women's Political Council (WPC) swung into action. The WPC, a group of black professional women in Montgomery, began organizing a bus boycott to coincide with Rosa's trial, which was set for Monday, December 5. Boycott organizers quickly wrote and printed up a handbill. "Another Negro woman has been arrested and thrown into jail," the handbill read, "because she refused to get up out of her seat on the bus and give it to a white person. . . . This woman's case will come up on Monday. We are, therefore, asking every Negro to stay off the buses in protest of the arrest and trial."

Because 75 percent of the people who used the buses in Montgomery were black, the boycott could dramatically reduce ridership—and with it the fares collected by the bus company. But for the boycott to succeed, it would have to be well publicized within the city's African American communities. In addition, blacks would have to be convinced to support the effort. Not riding the buses would cause many people serious inconvenience on a workday.

A meeting of black ministers was called for the evening of Friday, December 2, at the Dexter Avenue Baptist Church. If they agreed to speak about the boycott during Sunday services, perhaps the ministers could convince their congregations to participate. Rosa spoke at the Friday meeting. She told the ministers how she had been arrested. Although some did not want to get involved with the protest and left the meeting, others stayed and agreed to spread the word to their congregations. In addition, arrangements were made with black cab owners to pick up passengers along bus routes for 10 cents—the cost of a bus fare.

## The Boycott and the Trial

The morning of December 5, 1955, was dark and overcast, but an estimated 90 percent of Montgomery's African Americans participated in the bus boycott. The few who rode the buses either didn't know about the boycott or didn't want to be inconvenienced. Many in the latter group hid below the windows when their bus passed one of the large groups of blacks waiting patiently for a cab ride. African Americans had banded together to take a stand against the terrible practice of segregation.

That same morning, Rosa Parks arrived at the courthouse for her trial. A crowd of supporters had gathered, and one woman shouted out, "They've messed with the

Rosa Parks, seen here with E. D. Nixon (center) and attorney Fred Gray, was fined $10 and ordered to pay court costs for violating Montgomery's segregation ordinance for city buses.

The Rev. Martin Luther King Jr., head of the Montgomery Improvement Association (MIA), speaks to organizers of the bus boycott, January 1956. Rosa Parks is at center. To her right is the Rev. Ralph Abernathy, Dr. King's close adviser at the MIA.

wrong one now." Rosa pled not guilty. But as expected, she was found guilty of breaking the segregation laws of the town. Rosa's lawyers actually wanted the local courts to find her guilty, so they could appeal her case to a higher court, the first step toward changing segregation laws. Before she left the courthouse, Rosa was given a suspended sentence and fined $10.

That night, African American ministers and community leaders met to discuss extending the boycott. They formed an organization called the Montgomery Improvement Association (MIA). A young minister named Martin

READ MORE

For a brief profile of Martin Luther King Jr., see page 52.

Luther King Jr., pastor at the Dexter Avenue Baptist Church, was chosen as the MIA's president. Rosa Parks attended the meeting and heard Dr. King speak to the large group of African Americans who had gathered at the Holt Street Baptist Church. A decision had to be made: would the black community continue the boycott? "One of the great glories of democracy," King said, "is the right to protest for right. . . . [I]f you will protest courageously and yet with dignity and Christian love, when the history books are written in future generations the historians will pause and say, 'There lived a great people—the black people—who injected new meaning and dignity into the veins of civilization.'"

After King's eloquent speech, a vote was taken on whether to extend the boycott, with people asked to stand as a sign of a yes vote. At first a few stood, then a few more . . . until the entire gathering was on its feet and the people outside were yelling, "Yes!" The boycott would continue.

## The Long Boycott

In the months that followed, local police harassed African Americans who participated in the bus boycott. Many lost their jobs. Raymond Parks quit his job as a barber when his employer decreed that no one could speak of the boycott or of Rosa Parks. He was not going to stay at a place where he could not even mention his wife's name. Rosa herself was let go by the department store where she was employed as a seamstress on the pretext that there was no work for her to do.

To help the boycott, Rosa did jobs for the MIA. She helped collect and distribute clothing and, especially, shoes to those who needed them. Walking to work each day, people wore out their shoes very quickly. Churches collected enough money to purchase a few station wagons. Rosa even acted as a dispatcher by matching people needing rides with volunteer drivers. Some

African Americans in Montgomery walk to work, February 1956. An over-whelming majority of the city's blacks honored the bus boycott, causing the bus company—and downtown businesses—to lose a great deal of money.

employers who relied on their black employees even picked up their workers themselves. Soon an efficient transportation system had been worked out to provide about 30,000 African Americans with rides each workday.

Through all of this, blacks and the whites helping them received threatening letters and phone calls. The homes of Martin Luther King Jr. and the Rev. Ralph Abernathy, King's close assistant at the MIA, were both bombed. Police began stopping white drivers who had black passengers for minor traffic violations.

The boycott in Montgomery did not go unnoticed by the rest of the country. Stories on it were in all the papers, and by now

Rosa was famous. She was often asked to speak to churches and other organizations on the boycott and her experience on the bus.

## Legal Matters

With the boycott continuing, the bus company was losing money. So were the white merchants with stores in Montgomery's downtown area. In February 1956, an old law prohibiting boycotts was revived, leading to the arrest of Dr. King and other ministers and

Rosa Parks and E. D. Nixon arrive at the courthouse in Montgomery for the trial of Martin Luther King Jr., March 19, 1956. More than 150 people, including Rosa and Nixon, were arrested under a 1921 law that made it a crime to impede buses. But only Dr. King was tried. He was convicted.

leaders of the MIA. Rosa was also arrested. Ultimately, King was the only one tried. He was found guilty and ordered to pay a fine of $1,000 or face more than a year in jail. He refused to pay the fine and was put in jail, but his case was appealed and he was eventually set free.

During that same period, Rosa Parks's original conviction—for refusing to give her seat to the white passenger—was appealed, but the appeal was rejected. Rosa's attorney, Fred Gray, filed another suit on behalf of Rosa and four other women who had been mistreated on the bus. The suit claimed that bus segregation was unconstitutional. Gray and his clients, as well as the organizers of the boycott and the bus boycotters themselves, hoped that the case would eventually go to the U.S. Supreme Court. In June, the Court agreed to hear the case. It would take about five months before a decision would come down. Meanwhile, the boycott continued.

## Victory

On November 13, 1956, the Supreme Court handed down its decision: segregation on the Montgomery buses was unconstitutional. The bus boycott went on, however, until there was a written order implementing the Court's decision. That order arrived on December 20.

The next day, the boycott ended and the African American community in Montgomery, Alabama, returned to riding the buses. When Rosa boarded the bus for the first time, reporters and photographers from *Look* magazine were there to capture the moment. She took a seat, and one of the most famous photos of Rosa Parks was taken as she looked pensively out the window—perhaps thinking back on the past year and her part in the Montgomery bus boycott.

The civil rights movement was on its way.

Rosa boards a Montgomery bus on December 21, 1956, at the end of the bus boycott. Numerous photographers were on hand to witness the event.

# CHAPTER FIVE

---

# WORKING FOR CIVIL RIGHTS

---

The court-ordered desegregation of city buses didn't end the racial strife in Montgomery. There were several incidents in which blacks riding on the now-integrated buses were harassed and beaten. One black rider was shot. Snipers fired at buses. In addition, shots were fired into the home of Martin Luther King Jr., the homes of two other black ministers were bombed, and four African American churches were bombed. Montgomery city officials also did their best to inconvenience black bus riders and thereby limit integration on the buses. A new curfew was put into place so that buses were no longer allowed to run after 5 P.M. This meant, of course, that people who worked until five o'clock couldn't get home on the bus.

But Montgomery's black citizens held firm. Despite the inconvenience and intimidation, they continued riding the buses. Eventually the violence began to subside. In the meantime, another bus boycott was launched by African Americans in Tallahassee, Florida. In early 1957, Martin Luther King and other prominent black leaders formed the Southern Christian Leadership Conference (SCLC) to coordinate protests against segregation across the entire South. Later in the year, nine black students integrated Central High School in Little Rock, Arkansas. Federal troops were called in to ensure the students were admitted. The scope of the civil rights movement was rapidly widening.

## Moving to Detroit

Though the Montgomery bus boycott had ended, Rosa Parks continued to receive threatening phone calls. And sometimes angry whites confronted her face-to-face. Rosa and Raymond Parks began to feel uneasy living in Montgomery. In 1957, they decided to leave the dangerous atmosphere. Along with Rosa's mother, they moved to Detroit, Michigan, where Rosa's brother lived.

After the family was settled in Detroit, Rosa was offered a job at the Hampton Institute, a black college in Boston, Massachusetts. Although she accepted the job and moved to Hampton by herself, she missed her family. She eventually left Hampton and returned to Michigan. Rosa continued to travel and speak on behalf of the civil rights movement, which was growing.

By 1962, Martin Luther King Jr. and the Southern Christian Leadership Conference were campaigning for the civil rights of African Americans on a variety of fronts. King always advocated nonviolence, even when confronted with violent adversaries. Rosa Parks personally saw him put this philosophy in action when she attended an SCLC meeting in September 1962. At the meeting, a white man leaped onto the stage and began assaulting King. Instead of fighting back, King simply stood there and instructed that no one touch the attacker.

## The March on Washington

In 1963, President John F. Kennedy asked Congress to pass a federal civil rights bill. To show support for this bill and to send a message that the time had come for such legislation, the SCLC

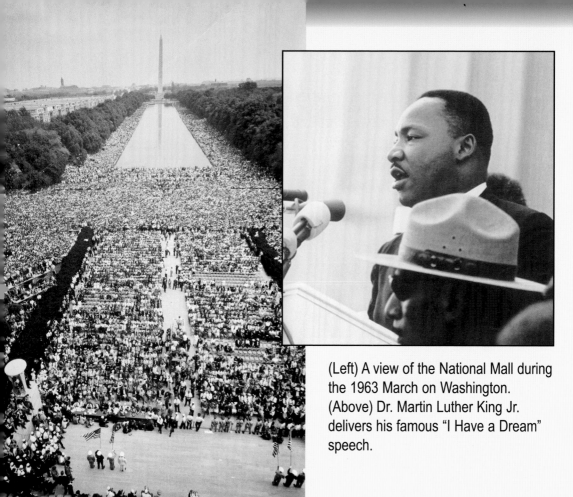

(Left) A view of the National Mall during the 1963 March on Washington. (Above) Dr. Martin Luther King Jr. delivers his famous "I Have a Dream" speech.

planned a march on Washington, D.C. In addition to the major African American organizations such as the NAACP and National Urban League, the march gained support from Jewish, Catholic, and Protestant leaders.

Unfortunately, the leaders of the march did not encourage women to participate. Rosa Parks and the wives of the leaders, such as Coretta Scott King, did not march with the group. Instead, a "Tribute to Women" was planned for the program, during which prominent African American women who were active in the civil rights movement would be introduced to the crowd. The famous black singer and dancer Josephine Baker was chosen to make the introductions. She introduced Rosa Parks, singers

Marian Anderson and Mahalia Jackson, and actress and singer Lena Horne. Rosa was not given the opportunity to speak.

There were speeches that day, however, and one stood out above all the others: Martin Luther King's "I Have a Dream" speech. The speech mesmerized the quarter million people who were gathered at the National Mall.

Following the assassination of President John F. Kennedy in November 1963, the Civil Rights Act of 1964 was passed and signed by President Lyndon B. Johnson on July 2, 1964. It was one of the most sweeping pieces of civil rights legislation in U.S. history. Among other provisions, the act outlawed discrimination based on race, religion, gender, or ethnicity in any facility open to the public (such as hotels, restaurants, theaters, and stores); prohibited discrimination in employment; and called for the

President Lyndon B. Johnson signs into law the landmark Civil Rights Act, July 2, 1964. Martin Luther King Jr. is directly behind the president.

desegregation of schools. The act also attempted to guarantee the voting rights of African Americans by requiring that the same standards, rules, and procedure be applied to everyone. For example, if African Americans were required to pass a literacy test in order to be registered to vote, whites were supposed to have to pass the same test.

# Fighting for Voter Rights

Despite the voting rights provisions of the Civil Rights Act, in many areas of the South state and local authorities continued to block African American citizens from exercising their right to vote. In some places, arbitrary limits were set on the number of people who were permitted to register. In other places, voter registration offices were simply closed without explanation. These measures primarily affected black voters because a much greater proportion of whites were already registered. And literacy tests and poll taxes continued to be a major barrier to registration for African American citizens.

The result was that in places such as Mississippi, Louisiana, and Alabama, rates of black-voter registration remained very low. In Selma, Alabama, for example, less than 2 percent of the eligible black population was registered to vote at the time of the 1964 elections.

In 1965, to focus public attention on the issue of voter rights, Martin Luther King organized a march from Selma to Montgomery. Six hundred marchers set off from Selma on March 7. Almost immediately, the marchers were attacked and dispersed by state troopers and local law officers firing tear gas and wielding billy clubs. Two weeks later—after a court order prohibiting police from stopping the march had been handed down—the demonstrators again set out from Selma, with Dr. King now leading about 3,200 marchers. Their numbers grew steadily along the 50-mile route to

Montgomery. By the time the march neared Montgomery, there were about 25,000 participants.

Rosa Parks had recently taken a job as an office aide and receptionist for John Conyers, a newly elected U.S. congressman from Detroit. But she traveled to Alabama to take part in the last leg of the march to Montgomery. Rosa was now 52 years old. Almost 10 years had passed since the Montgomery bus boycott, and many of the young marchers didn't know who she was. She kept getting pulled out of the march because she wasn't wearing the designated colors of the marchers. But then someone would recognize her and invite her back into the group.

On March 25, when the marchers finally reached their destination—the state capitol building in Montgomery—they were met by a crowd of screaming white demonstrators. The entire march, including attacks against the marchers, had been thoroughly documented by the media. Many Americans were shocked and

On the road to Montgomery, 1965. The march from Selma to the Alabama state capital focused attention on the issue of voting rights.

angered by the violence. Public opinion increasingly favored the cause of civil rights.

On August 6, 1965, President Johnson signed the Voting Rights Act of 1965. It was another landmark piece of civil rights legislation. The act completely prohibited the use of literacy tests as a means of determining voter eligibility. It also gave the federal government broad authority to enforce fair voting practices in the states—thereby breaking the power of state and local authorities to exclude black voters through corrupt and illegal means. Eleven years earlier, Rosa Parks had helped spark the civil rights movement with her courageous act on a Montgomery bus. Although she was not among the invited guests when President Johnson signed the Voting Rights Act into law at the U.S. Capitol, Rosa had done much to make the historic event possible.

## Losses

In April 1968, Martin Luther King was assassinated in Memphis, Tennessee. Rosa attended the great civil rights leader's funeral, which was held in Atlanta, Georgia. She had come to know Dr. King during the Montgomery bus boycott.

Rosa experienced a string of personal losses over the following decade. Both her husband, Raymond, and her brother, Sylvester, died of cancer in 1977. In 1979, Rosa's mother, Leona McCauley, passed away at the age of 91.

## Still Working to Make a Difference

In 1987, Rosa fulfilled a dream that she and her husband had discussed while he was still alive. She cofounded the Rosa and Raymond Parks Institute for Self-Development. The institute—whose mission is to help young people fulfill their potential through a variety of multicultural and cross-generational programs—offers courses in communication skills, economic skills, political awareness, and health awareness.

In September 1988, a year after establishing the Rosa and Raymond Parks Institute, Rosa retired from her position in the office of Representative John Conyers. She'd been working for the congressman for more than 20 years. One of Rosa's jobs during that time had been to find housing for homeless people in Conyers's congressional district.

**READ MORE**

For additional information about the Rosa and Raymond Parks Institute for Self-Development, turn to page 53.

Though now 75 years old, Rosa stayed busy. In 1992, she published her first book—an autobiography titled *Rosa Parks: My Story*. Two years later, Rosa published *Quiet Strength*, a memoir geared toward younger readers.

In October 1995, the Million Man March was held. The huge event—which took place in Washington, D.C.—was conceived

The civil rights icon reads from her book *I Am Rosa Parks* at the launch of a summer and after-school program in Detroit, July 1, 1997.

as a way to promote unity and responsibility among African American men. Because of its size and its location, the Million Man March was somewhat reminiscent of 1963's March on Washington. At the 1995 event, however, Rosa Parks was asked to give a speech. When she got up to speak, the crowd chanted her name, loudly paying tribute to this civil rights icon.

Rosa also spoke at smaller events. Not having any children of her own, she especially enjoyed her visits to elementary schools, where she spoke of the past and her hope for the future. "We still have a long way to go," Rosa said in 1995, "but we still have many obstacles and many challenges to face. It's far from perfect, and it may never be, but I think as long as we do the best we can to improve conditions, then people will be benefited."

Rosa was the recipient of many awards and honorary degrees. In 1996, President Bill Clinton gave her the Presidential Medal of Freedom, the nation's highest civilian award.

Rosa Parks with President Bill Clinton, June 15, 1999. The occasion was a Capitol Hill ceremony at which Rosa was presented with the Congressional Gold Medal.

The Mother of the Civil Rights Movement, 1999.

# Passing of a Civil Rights Icon

Rosa Parks died on October 24, 2005. She was 92 years old. Her body was flown to Washington, D.C., where it lay in state at the Capitol Rotunda. Rosa was the first woman to be accorded that honor. Thirty thousand visitors filed past her casket to pay their last respects to the civil rights leader who embodied quiet strength. Across the country, Americans honored the enormous contribution that this simple Southern woman made for equality and justice. By living example, she showed that the act of one human being can ripple through the years and bring great change for the good of millions of people.

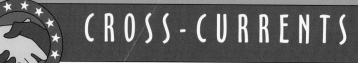

# Freeing the Slaves

President Abraham Lincoln issued the Emancipation Proclamation on January 1, 1863. It declared that all persons being held in slavery in the rebellious Confederate states were now free and would always be free.

Despite this bold statement, the Emancipation Proclamation was actually limited in scope. It didn't free slaves in border states that remained loyal to the Union, because Lincoln didn't want people in these states to become angry and join the Confederacy. Also, as a practical matter, slaves could only be set free in the South after Union troops conquered territory. But the Emancipation Proclamation allowed freed slaves to fight in the Union army and navy, and as many as 200,000 did.

As the Civil War wound down, some people were concerned that the Emancipation Proclamation would not permanently end slavery. So they pushed for an amendment to the U.S. Constitution. In January 1865, Congress passed the Thirteenth Amendment, which stated: "Neither slavery nor involuntary servitude . . . shall exist within the United States." When the amendment was ratified in December 1865, slavery in the United States was officially ended.

Lincoln signing the Emancipation Proclamation.

# The Jim Crow Laws

The Fourteenth Amendment to the Constitution, ratified in 1868, guaranteed blacks full citizenship and equal protection under the law. The Fifteenth Amendment, ratified in 1870, gave black men the right to vote. Nevertheless, Southern states passed local laws that segregated blacks from whites and made African Americans second-class citizens in their communities.

These regulations were known as the Jim Crow laws. The name came from a character depicting an offensive stereotype of African Americans in song-and-dance shows from the mid-1800s. Each Southern state had its own version of Jim Crow laws. But the goal was the same: to restrict the lives of African Americans and keep blacks away from whites.

The Jim Crow laws made blacks and whites attend separate schools, ride separate trains and buses, stay in separate hotels, eat at separate restaurants, use separate public bathrooms, even drink at separate water fountains. Although the facilities provided for blacks were supposed to be as good as those provided for whites, they weren't.

This treatment of African Americans as second-class citizens became a way of life for people in the South, both black and white. And it would continue from the mid-1870s all the way into the 1960s.

Jim Crow, the minstrel-show character after which Southern segregation laws were named.

# CROSS-CURRENTS

## The Ku Klux Klan

In 1866, a group of Confederate Civil War veterans in Pulaski, Tennessee, founded the Ku Klux Klan, or KKK. At first the KKK was just a small, local social club. But it soon grew into a large, powerful organization that was dedicated to keeping African Americans from claiming their rights. Across the South, Klan members terrorized blacks, as well as whites sympathetic to African Americans. Often striking at night, the KKK burned houses and pulled people from their beds to beat or murder them. Victims' bodies were frequently left hanging from trees as a warning that blacks should "stay in their place." To keep from being recognized, Klan members wore white robes and hoods that covered their faces and heads.

In 1871, Congress passed the Force Bill, which gave the federal government broad powers to suppress the KKK's activities. The violence against freedmen finally subsided, though it did not end completely.

In the early 1900s, the Klan had a resurgence. But this time, Klan members didn't just target African Americans. They also directed their violence toward other ethnic and religious groups, such as new immigrants, Jews, and Roman Catholics. A burning cross in front of the homes of victims became the new Klan's calling card.

By the 1940s, the membership and influence of the Ku Klux Klan had dwindled, but there was a short revival of the Klan during the civil rights movement of the 1950s and 1960s.

A Ku Klux Klan rally, circa 1925.

## The Scottsboro Boys

On March 25, 1931, a dozen African American youths between the ages of 13 and 19 hopped on a freight train in Alabama. Also on the train were some young white men and two white women. A fight broke out, and all but one of the white men as well as three of the black youths were thrown from the train. None were seriously hurt. But when the train arrived at the next station, the police were waiting for the remaining nine black youths. It was then that the two white women leveled an explosive charge: that the nine black teens had raped them. The blacks were arrested and taken to the county seat of Scottsboro, Alabama.

The white women were given medical exams, which showed no evidence that they had been raped. Nevertheless, the young men—now known as the "Scottsboro Boys"—were quickly tried and found guilty by all-white juries. All but the youngest, a 13-year-old, was sentenced to death.

The Scottsboro Boys case created outrage throughout much of the country. Rallies were held, and legal appeals were filed. The teens were granted a new trial in March 1933. By this time, one of the alleged victims admitted that she and the other woman had made up the entire story about being raped. Still, the Scottsboro Boys were again convicted. Another round of appeals and trials produced the same result later in 1933. The four youngest defendants were finally pardoned in 1936, but the remaining Scottsboro Boys weren't released until the mid-1940s.

The Scottsboro boys in jail, consulting with their lawyer.

# Brown v. Board of Education

In May of 1954, the Supreme Court handed down its decision in a landmark civil rights case, *Brown v. Board of Education* of Topeka. The case upheld the goal of the Fourteenth Amendment to the Constitution, which guaranteed citizens equal protection of the laws. In *Brown v. Board of Education*, the Supreme Court ruled that children could not be assigned and restricted to schools according to their race.

Under local Jim Crow laws, states had skirted the issue of equality by passing laws that kept blacks and whites segregated. An 1896 Supreme Court decision, *Plessy v. Ferguson*, had held racial segregation to be legal, as long as the separate facilities provided to blacks and whites were equal. "Separate but equal" had thus become the accepted legal standard.

Of course, the facilities provided to African Americans were invariably not equal, but inferior. *The Brown v. Board of Education* decision acknowledged this fact. While the case centered on the right of African American families to send their children to white schools, the decision would undercut the legal basis for segregation in all areas of society.

The plaintiffs in the *Brown v. Board of Education* case.

# The NAACP

The NAACP is one of the country's most prominent civil rights organizations. Its mission is "to ensure the political, educational, social, and economic equality of rights of all persons and to eliminate racial hatred and racial discrimination."

In 1908, several thousand whites attacked a black community in Springfield, Illinois. The mob shot innocent people, looted stores, burned homes, and lynched two elderly African Americans. Following this race riot, a group of African Americans and concerned whites banded together to form an organization that would try to protect the rights of black people. The National Association for the Advancement of Colored People, or NAACP, was founded on February 12, 1909. A national office was established in New York City the following year.

Ending the practice of lynching was one of the NAACP's early priorities. In 1918, the organization helped convince President Woodrow Wilson publicly to declare lynching evil. By the following year, the NAACP's membership stood at about 90,000.

In 1940, the NAACP Legal Defense and Educational Fund was founded to help poor minority defendants. Led by its director, Thurgood Marshall, the Legal Defense and Educational Fund would be instrumental in bringing the *Brown v. Board of Education* case before the Supreme Court. Marshall would go on to become a Supreme Court justice himself.

Today, with more than half a million members, the NAACP continues to be a major advocate for equality.

# Martin Luther King Jr.

As a young pastor, Martin Luther King Jr. led the successful Montgomery bus boycott. Over the next dozen years, he would become the civil rights movement's most prominent leader. In 1964, Dr. King was awarded the Nobel Peace Prize for his fight against racial injustice.

King's practice of nonviolence had its roots in his deep Christian faith. Born in Atlanta, Georgia, in 1929, he grew up in the Ebenezer Baptist Church, where his father was the pastor. After graduating from Morehouse College and Crozer Theological Seminary, King was ordained a Baptist minister at the age of 19. He became Ebenezer's associate pastor. After marrying Coretta Scott in 1953, he became pastor of the Dexter Avenue Baptist Church in Montgomery. He later received his doctorate degree in theology from Boston University.

In 1968, Dr. King was assassinated by a white supremacist. A quarter century later, the U.S. Congress established a national holiday to honor him. Today, Martin Luther King Jr. Day is celebrated on the third Monday of every January. It is a day that reminds everyone of King's hopeful dream: "when all of God's children, black men and white men, Jews and Gentiles, Protestants and Catholics, will be able to join hands and sing . . . 'Free at last, free at last. Thank God Almighty, we are free at last.'"

Martin Luther King Jr.

# The Rosa and Raymond Parks Institute for Self-Development

The Rosa and Raymond Parks Institute was founded in 1987 by Rosa Parks and her close friend Elaine Eason Steele. The institute, located in Detroit, provides hands-on and intergenerational learning experiences for people of all ages. But it never strays far from the goals of the young Rosa Parks, who worked as an NAACP volunteer, helping people reach their potential by recognizing their own power as individuals.

One of the institute's most popular programs is "Pathways to Freedom." Conducted on local, regional, and national levels, the five-week summer program takes students to sites where historic events occurred. Some of these places include stops along the Underground Railroad, where escaping slaves during the 1800s were helped by both black and white citizens who opposed slavery.

The Rosa and Raymond Parks Institute's intergenerational learning programs bring seniors and young people together. The young people teach the seniors skills such as how to use a computer. The seniors, in turn, impart lessons they have learned during their lives.

# Chronology

**1913:** Rosa Louise McCauley is born on February 4, in Tuskegee, Alabama.

**1925:** Attends Miss White's Industrial School for Girls in Montgomery, Alabama; drops out in 1929 to care for her ill grandmother.

**1932:** Marries Raymond Parks, a barber and civil rights activist, in December.

**1934:** Earns her high school diploma at age 20.

**1941:** Gets a job at Maxwell Air Force Base, an integrated military station.

**1943:** Joins the NAACP as a volunteer secretary to E. D. Nixon.

**1945:** Passes literacy test and registers to vote for the first time.

**1955:** Attends leadership workshops at the Highlander School in Tennessee. On December 1, refuses to give up her seat on a bus to a white passenger and is arrested. On December 5, stands trial and is found guilty. On the same day, the Montgomery bus boycott starts in protest of Rosa's arrest; the boycott is a success as African Americans stay off the buses.

**1956:** In January, Rosa loses her job working as a seamstress at the Montgomery Fair department store. On February 21, Rosa is again arrested for being part of the boycott; charges are dropped. The bus boycott ends on December 21, after the Supreme Court rules in favor of ending segregation on buses in Montgomery.

**1957:** Rosa and her husband and mother move to Detroit, Michigan.

**1963:** Attends the March on Washington on August 28; Martin Luther King delivers his famous "I Have a Dream" speech at that event.

**1965:** Rosa begins working for Congressman John Conyers. In March, she participates in the march from Selma to Montgomery for voter rights. City of Montgomery changes the street name of Cleveland Avenue to Rosa Parks Boulevard.

**1968:** Martin Luther King Jr. is assassinated on April 4.

**1977:** Rosa's husband, Raymond, and her brother, Sylvester, both die of cancer.

**1979:** Leona McCauley, Rosa's mother, dies.

**1987:** Rosa establishes the Rosa and Raymond Parks Institute for Self-Development.

**1988:** Retires from Congressman Conyers's office.

**1992:** Publishes her first book, an autobiography titled *Rosa Parks: My Story*.

**1995:** Speaks at the Million Man March held in Washington, D.C.

**2005:** Dies in Detroit, Michigan, at the age of 92.

# Accomplishments and Awards

## Awards

Spingarn Medal, highest award from the NAACP, 1979

Martin Luther King Jr. Nonviolent Peace Prize, 1980

Service Award, *Ebony*, 1980

The Eleanor Roosevelt Women of Courage Award, 1984

Ellis Island Medal of Honor, 1986

Martin Luther King Jr. Leadership Award, 1987

Adam Clayton Powell Jr. Legislative Achievement Award, 1990

Rosa Parks Peace Prize, 1994

Presidential Medal of Freedom, 1996

International Freedom Conductor's Award, National Underground
Railroad Freedom Center, 1998

Detroit-Windsor International Freedom Festival Freedom Award, 1999

U.S. Congressional Gold Medal, 1999

Governor's Medal of Honor for Extraordinary Courage, Alabama,
2000

Gandhi, King, Ikeda Award for peace, 2002

## Published Books

*Rosa Parks: My Story* with Jim Haskins, 1992

*Quiet Strength*, 1994

*Dear Mrs. Parks: A Dialogue with Today's Youth* with Gregory J. Reed,
1996

*I Am Rosa Parks* with Jim Haskins, 1997

# Further Reading

Davis, Kenneth. *Don't Know Much About: Rosa Parks*. New York: HarperCollins Publishers, 2005.

Parks, Rosa. *Quiet Strength*. Grand Rapids, Mich.: Zondervan, 1994

Parks, Rosa, with Jim Haskins. *Rosa Parks: My Story*. New York: Puffin Books, 1992.

Venable, Rose. *The Civil Rights Movement*. Chanhassen, Minn.: The Child's World, 2002.

# Internet Resources

http://www.naacp.org

> The official Web site of the NAACP.

http://www.jimcrowhistory.org

> This educators' site, called "The History of Jim Crow," explores the history of segregation in the United States, from the 1870s through the 1950s.

http://pbs.org/wnet/aaworld/timeline.html

> This Public Broadcasting Service Web site presents a timeline of the African American experience.

# Glossary

**activist**—someone who works hard to bring about social or political change.

**appeals**—formal requests to have a court decision reviewed by a higher court.

**boycott**—to refuse to buy a product, use a service, or patronize an establishment as a means of protest.

**integrated**—having people of different racial backgrounds working and living together in the same place.

**lynching**—the killing of a person suspected of a crime before he or she has a fair trial; usually carried out by a mob.

**naturalized**—given citizenship in a country not of one's birth.

**plaintiff**—in a court of law, the person who brings a lawsuit against another person or organization.

**theology**—the study of religion and religious beliefs.

**unconstitutional**—not supported by or in conflict with the Constitution (and thus illegal).

**watershed**—an important turning point in history.

# Chapter Notes

p. 8: "I suspect that . . ." Rosa Parks, *Rosa Parks: My Story* (New York: Puffin Books, 1992), 159.

p. 9: "that all Men are . . ." Declaration of Independence.

p. 12: "deprive any person of life . . ." 14th Amendment to the U.S. Constitution, http://www.nps.gov/archive/malu/documents/amend14.htm

p. 16: "I was very much . . ." Parks, *My Story*, 23.

p. 18: "that I was a person . . ." Ibid., 49.

p. 18: "person who inspired . . ." Rosa Parks Interview, Pioneer of Civil Rights, June 2, 1995, Williamsburg, Virginia. http://achievement.org/autodoc/page/par0int-3

p. 22: "Get off . . ." Parks, *My Story*, 79.

p. 22: " You better not . . ." Ibid.

p. 22: "How come . . ." Ibid.

p. 24: "Black people . . ." Mary Hull, *Rosa Parks: Civil Rights Leader* (Philadelphia: Chelsea House Publishers, 1994), 60.

p. 25: "Your ancestors will . . ." The Murder of Emmett Till, PBS *American Experience* documentary. http://www.pbs.org/wgbh/amex/till/peopleevents/e_trial.html

p. 26: "You may . . ." Parks, *My Story*, 116.

p. 26: "I [had] made up . . ." Rosa Parks Interview.

p. 28: "Another Negro . . ." Parks, *My Story*, 126.

p. 29: "They've messed . . ." Ibid., 133.

p. 31: "One of the great . . ." Ibid., 138.

p. 44: "We still have . . ." Rosa Parks Interview.

p. 46: "Neither slavery nor . . ." 13th Amendment to the U.S. Constitution. http://www.nps.gov/archive/malu/documents/amend13.htm

p. 51: "to ensure the political . . ." NAACP Web site. About the NAACP. Our Mission. http://naacp.org/about/mission/index.htm

p. 52: "when all of . . ." "I Have a Dream Speech" transcript. http://www.stanford.edu/group/King/publications/speeches/address_at_march_on_washington.pdf

# Index

Abernathy, Ralph, *30*, 32
African Americans
 attacks on, 15–16, 32, 36, 40–42,
  48, 51
 and education, 12, 14–15, 17–18,
  37, 40, 50
 and voter rights, 22–24, 40–42, 47
 *See also* segregation
Alabama State Teachers' College for
 Negroes, 18
amendments (Constitution), 11, 12,
 46, 47, 50
Anderson, Marian, 23, 39

Baker, Josephine, 38–39
Black Codes, 11–12
 *See also* Jim Crow laws
Booker T. Washington Junior High,
 18
*Brown v. Board of Education*, 24, 50,
 51
 *See also* segregation
bus boycott
 Florida, 36
 Montgomery, 6–8, 28–35, 36

Civil Rights Act of 1866, 11–12
Civil Rights Act of 1964, 39–40
civil rights movement, 8, 27, 36–37
 and legislation, 11–12, 37–38,
  39–40, 42
 and the March on Washington,
  37–39, 44
 and the Million Man March,
  43–44
 and the National Association for
  the Advancement of Colored
  People (NAACP), 18, 20–21, 25,
  27, 38, 51

and the Selma march, 40–42
and the Southern Christian
 Leadership Conference (SCLC),
 36, 37–38
*See also* voting rights
Civil War, 11, *12*, 46
Clinton, Bill, 44
Constitution, 9–10, 11, 12, 22, 46,
 47, 50
Conyers, John, 41, 43

desegregation. *See* segregation
Durr, Clifford, 24, 26
Durr, Virginia, 24, 26

education, 12, 14–15, 16, 17–18, 37,
 40, 50
Emancipation Proclamation, 11, 46

Fifteenth Amendment, 47
Force Bill, 48
Fourteenth Amendment, 12, 47, 50
Freedmen's Bureau, 12

Gray, Fred, *29*, 34

Hampton Institute, 37
Highlander Folk School conference,
 24–25
Horne, Lena, 39
Horton, Myles, 24

"I Have a Dream" speech, *38*, 39
 *See also* King, Martin Luther, Jr.

Jackson, Mahalia, 39
Jim Crow laws, 12, *14*, 17, 20, 47, 50
 *See also* segregation
Johnson, Lyndon B., 39, 42

Numbers in **bold italics** refer to captions.

Kennedy, John F., 37, 39
King, Coretta Scott, 38, 52
King, Martin Luther, Jr., *7*, 30–31,
    32, 33–34, 36, 37, 52
  assassination of, 42
  "I Have a Dream" speech, *38*, 39
  and the Selma voting rights
    march, 40–41
  *See also* civil rights movement
Ku Klux Klan, 15–16, 48

Lincoln, Abraham, 11, 46

March on Washington, 37–39, 44
Marshall, Thurgood, 51
Martin Luther King Jr. Day, 52
  *See also* King, Martin Luther, Jr.
Maxwell Field Army Air Force base,
    20
McCauley, James (father), 13
McCauley, Leona Edwards (mother),
    13, 16, 17, 18, 37, 42
McCauley, Rosa Louise. *See* Parks,
    Rosa
McCauley, Sylvester (brother),
    13–14, 16, 37, 42
Million Man March, 43–44
Montgomery, Alabama, 16–17,
    21–22, 25–27, 37, 40–42
  bus boycott in, 6–8, 28–35, 36
Montgomery Improvement
    Association (MIA), 30–32, 34
Montgomery Industrial School (Miss
    White's School for Girls), 17–18
Montgomery Voters League, 23–24

NAACP Youth Council, 21
National Association for the
    Advancement of Colored People
    (NAACP), 18, 20–21, 25, 27, 38,
    51
National Urban League, 38
Nixon, E. D., 21, 26, *29*, *33*

Parks, Raymond, 18–19, 26, 31, 37,
    42
Parks, Rosa
  arrests of, 25, 26–27, *33*, 34
  as author, 43
  awards and honors won by, 44
  birth of, 13

and childhood, 13–18
  as aide to John Conyers, 41, 43
  death of, 45
  and education, 14–15, 16, 17–18
  at the Hampton Institute, 37
  at the Highlander Folk School
    conference, 24–25
  and the March on Washington,
    38–39
  marriage of, to Raymond Parks,
    18–19
  and the Million Man March,
    43–44
  and the Montgomery bus boycott,
    6–8, 28–35, 36
  move of, to Detroit, 37
  joins the NAACP, 20–21, 25
  and the Rosa and Raymond
    Parks Institute for Self-
    Development, 42–43, 53
  as secretary at Maxwell Field, 20
  and the Selma march, 41–42
  trial of, 29–30, 34
  and voting rights, 23–24
  work of, in the cotton fields,
    13–14
  *See also* civil rights movement
*Plessy v. Ferguson*, 50
  *See also* segregation
poll taxes, 23, 40
  *See also* voting rights

*Quiet Strength* (Parks), 43

Roosevelt, Eleanor, 23
Roosevelt, Franklin D., 20, 23
Rosa and Raymond Parks Institute
    for Self-Development, 42–43, 53
*Rosa Parks: My Story* (Parks), 43

Scottsboro Boys, 19, 49
segregation, 12, 13, 17, 20–22,
    25–27, 47
  and education, 14–15, 24, 37, 40,
    50
  and military bases, 20
  and the Montgomery bus boycott,
    6–8, 28–35, 36
Selma march, 40–42
slavery, 8–12, 46
Southern Christian Leadership

Conference (SCLC), 36, 37–38
   *See also* King, Martin Luther, Jr.
Steele, Elaine Eason, 53
Supreme Court, 6, 8, 24, 34, 50, 51

Thirteenth Amendment, 11, 46
Till, Emmett, 25
Tuskegee Institute, 13

voting rights, 22–24, 40–42, 47
   *See also* civil rights movement
Voting Rights Act of 1965, 42

White, Alice L., 17
Wilson, Woodrow, 51
Women's Political Council (WPC), 28

# Photo Credits

# About the Author

SUSAN HOE is an editor/writer who has worked on nonfiction books for children and young adults. These titles cover a wide range of subjects, including maps, wild animals, biographies, American history, and science. Susan and her husband currently live in the Phoenix area of Arizona.